The Unspoken Reflection

Reflection

Heal, Love, Prosper

By: April Nneka Okorie

ISBN-13: 978-1519259141

ISBN-10: 151925914X

This is one of many passages I wrote during a period of depression and self-hate. I wrote this during my ninth-grade year of high school. I was bullied throughout my school years, but ninth grade was when it reached another level that shook me to a point of no return.

May 13, 2013

I don't know what I hate more: the people who openly hate me and continue to harass me, or the people who secretly hate me but act like they don't. I want to write out my feelings because they always say it helps. I guess the theme of my writing today is pain because that is all I have been feeling lately. I barely have clear eyes anymore, and I never smile. My heart, my life, is just pain.

I keep feeling like I'm falling down for some reason. My pain just keeps getting worse. It's no longer only at school; the pain I feel follows me and haunts me even outside of school now. I wake up screaming and crying in the middle of the night, but I guess my family is immune to it since they sleep through it nowadays, except for my mother. "It's just that their words keep haunting me, Mommy," I keep telling her every night. These people claim they don't care about me and I am irrelevant but keep making my life miserable. Are they happy now?

It's really funny—today at school, I lost another friend! And her words were, "I can't be friends with you anymore. You get into too much drama." I basically get this every day or have people avoid me because they're scared it will mess up their reputation. But with her, I poured my heart to her, told her what they did to me. I really thought she cared for me the most, and now I lost her because it's getting worse? I wish she knew that if she was also being bullied, I wouldn't have stopped being friends with her. But who needs friends…ha.

No one truly even knows me, and they keep treating me this way. I hate myself for not allowing my mom to report my harassers to the school board. Was I scared? No, but I believed that it will never get better for me.

Every single day of my life that I decide to wake up and go to school is and will be the worst day of my life.

APRIL OKORIE is a self-love advocate. She published this book at

seventeen years of age in hopes of impacting individuals all over the world. With,

"The Unspoken Reflection: Heal, Love, Prosper," she hopes to touch individuals

who need guidance and a sense of understanding of the self. A former victim of

bullying, April changed her life into positivity. She has many passions including

sewing, designing, engaging in scientific research and reading. Her main mantra is,

"I am not *living* unless I do what I love, but I have not *lived* unless I touch a lost

soul that will spark the brain of another."

"When we make peace with ourselves, we naturally, progressively become aware of our spirit. Our spirit is our core, the thriving part of us. We don't have to go looking for it, because it is always with us. Each time period in our life has a meaning, a meaning that will shape our identity or build it. The advancement of spirit allows us to choose the direction we want with our life and how we choose to view the world. Clean your soul, do not allow the world to destroy your heart. Build yourself; love yourself and the people around you. Cure your being and free your mind from the morals that do not coexist with yours. Be yourself, treat your body, mind, and soul correctly and prosperity will come... I choose me today, I choose to heal. I choose to love. I choose to prosper."

---- The Unspoken Reflection: Heal, Love, Prosper

The natural instinct of people who seek to cleanse their soul is to become a better person. People who want to do so seek self-empowerment, but they do not go deep into the core of their mind, body, and soul in order to find their true meaning. In "The Unspoken Reflection: Heal, Love, Prosper", April Okorie takes people on a quest to help them find their true essence. The book contains three main perspectives and steps to help readers discover their true selves; the steps include healing, loving, and prospering. Each section will allow readers to gain understanding of the concept of patience. Each individual is different, and each individual will be able to decipher each aspect of the book that personally helps them. It all starts with the thought of self-sovereignty. Wanting to be a better person is not just a phrase; it is an action that takes patience and true comprehension. It is important to gain perspective and switch the direction of your mentality. The end of the book contains some of April's personal poetry, spoken words, and other writings that she felt she should share with the world.

<u>Table of Contents</u>

Heal: *What Your Mind Wants vs. What Your Soul Needs*

"The scarcity of self-acceptance is caused by the compulsion to be accepted by everyone else except ourselves. I want to heal for the benefit of my health, truth, and humanity; I must never be afraid to put myself first in order to truly heal"

-April Okorie

Sometimes I study birds and how they migrate to different destinations, whether their reason for leaving is happiness, sadness, discomfort, or discovery. Despite, the constant nomadic behavior, they have no control or knowledge of what the future has in store. Although I am human, birds once reflected my life, like the birds, I also was uncertain about what awaited me in life. I would always sit and ponder on my truth; but I always masked it and stayed in a state of personal discomfort in order to make people around me comfortable. The thought of remaining in the same position often haunts us, but we tend to correlate the mentality of "same position" with physical stagnation when they are polar opposites. They are polar opposites because one is mental, the other is physical. That is often the confusion with the concept of moving on in life: we believe it is physical when it is mental. Everything in the ideology of moving forward requires a mental change; we must cure our mind of things that keep us mentally motionless.

Our life is a series of steps with rules that are simple to follow: nurturing and cleanliness. The body needs food, water, and vitamins to keep us growing from infancy to childhood to adolescence to adulthood. It also needs to be cleansed with showers, and covered with clean garments. We follow those rules because we want to stay alive; we want to secure our sanity and fuel our body.

Why don't we take care of our inner body as we do our outer one? We do not think about others before we feel the need to wash the dirt off our body. We do not think of others when we are dying to eat our favorite meal. Why aren't we dying to feed, clean, and secure our soul? The answer is because we may never have been taught to do so. Our mind is susceptible to outside influence; we were taught that specific foods carry a certain amount of vitamins that will help us survive, but we were never taught to heal the damage of not knowing our worth. There comes a point in life where we have to start teaching ourselves things that provide us nourishment both physically and mentally. Health works both ways: changing your diet and lifestyle does not mean anything if you allow dirt and harshness to exist in your soul. Clearing your mind, body, and soul *is* health.

I was always bullied growing up, but the harassment level reached a higher level at the beginning of high school. The amount of verbal abuse I received from others was enough to destroy me for eternity. I was different, a loner, socially awkward, and could never connect with people; these attributes, which I had no control over, put me in the path toward being harassed. To this day I still think about the past, and whenever I look back, I feel numb. Exactly two years ago, I felt nothing but sadness and hopelessness. I questioned why I never healed while seeking acceptance from others. I basked in pretentious love, pretentious friendships, and pretentious happiness. The perception of being happy made my heart sick; it was filled with the dirt of social acceptance. It could not be true happiness if those I believed to be my genuine friends were not.

I am a very confident and secure individual now. I do not show anger to anyone who has ever neglected me, hurt me, used me, or made my soul feel lost in the past. I do not have a revenge mentality and I have not internalized a grudge against anyone. Instead, I show gratitude. I forgive everyone who taught me a lesson that I was destined to learn. The biggest adversity was dealing with the depression, stress, and anger I had inside. I listened to the words of others every day and defined myself by them. I was blinded by toxicity because I wanted to prove to the people that bullied me that I was good enough. I knew that I was the only person that could rid my heart of self-doubt; I had to realize that I too, am worthy. This is why I started to do right by my soul, meaning that I did whatever it took to cleanse, heal, and grow, even when it was painful and uncomfortable.

We never try to fully understand the root of negativity and why others are constantly damaging us. We blame ourselves and believe we are in the wrong for the way others act toward us. The automatic assumption is the idea that negativity rooted in the world is our biggest suppressor, but any form of negativity originating from others is not our fault. When animosity is geared toward us, it is never our business. It is the business of the oppressor because it is their conscience that is doing the damage.

Negativity is a way of expressing fear. The ones who spew negativity are afraid to be themselves. They push away their own persona by making others feel pain; this is due to someone else pushing them away at some point in their life. Whether it is adversity, failure, or upbringing that causes someone to be negative toward others, the cycle repeats itself. The cycle is the ongoing notion of pushing away someone's identity to make up for the inner torture they feel inside. They do not want people to be too happy, too expressive, or too "different" because society's biggest fear is individualism.

Individualism scares others; it singles out our differences and defies all laws of normality. It is the world's strongest force, because the power of being ourselves is so strong that it causes our adversity, happiness, success, and defeat. One must be willing to fight to be their truest form on earth. One must also be willing to accept that it is not the concept of "who is going to allow you to do something," it is the awareness and understanding of "who is going to stop me from doing what needs to be done."

There are three main steps to healing:

- Guilt

- Freedom

- Acceptance

Guilt

Being hungry for success requires working very hard, facing multiple obstacles, and needing the goal to succeed as much as breathing. Often times, people strive to be successful, and when the goal is achieved, some people make statements like, "Success is the best revenge". We say such things involuntarily; we attach our minds to the people who harmed us without even knowing it. We are not aware that we are still thinking about the people who hurt us mentally, physically, or spiritually. They linger in our thoughts and control our future actions, causing them to intertwine with our destiny.

Who are you trying to prove yourself to? Are you proving to yourself that everything you have accomplished should be reduced to the approval of people who are not even thinking of the harm they caused you? Are you trying to prove to yourself that you cannot be happy until people see that you are happy? This is called seeking self-validation through others and one will never heal with guilt in their soul. By saying vengeful statements, you are guilty of being emotionally attached to the people who are now the authority over your own life and successes. The past is still playing a huge role in your current life.

Be secure in yourself. Do not be guilty of having your worth depend on the opinions of others. If you achieve something and the people who harmed you now praise you, will that make you happy? They know they have a hold over your life because they determined your happiness. Never live your life or achieve things for the approval, fame, attention, or applause. Live your own life because you are doing things that make your individualism flourish. Internal happiness will begin to be reflected in your external happiness. You should and will be secure. Regardless of the applause or hatred you receive from others. Guilt can be erased with the desire to claim your identity and the energy to make your life about you. Once you get over the guilty pleasure of proving things to others, the first step of healing is mastered.

Freedom

It is better to be free than to not be free, but breaking the chain of emotional enslavement comes with perseverance and consistency. Shielded progress made under the vision of society, people, and expectations other than your own is false progression. It is hard to truly fly when something is weighing you down. Freedom is the ability to respond when needed. You do not have to say yes when society says it is OK. You do not have to surround yourself with people who make it uncomfortable to say no. You can go beyond the expected view of human perception to be free. This can be problematic, because there will always be something or someone that will block you from progressing.

In the past, I was very uncomfortable with everything regarding my life. I wanted everything to stay the way it was "supposed" to be," because I was used to people viewing me a certain way. I did not want to progress, because I was afraid that people would tell me that I had "changed" or that I had the un-fathomable perception of believing I was better than everyone else. I was between the desire to be free and the habit of acting the same way when that was not truly who I was. The people I surrounded myself with believed they knew me when they actually did not know a thing about who I am or who I was becoming.

The moment I broke the chain to reach for freedom, I was more alive and most of all, happy. I was tired of the constant withdrawal and questioning why I could not be myself. It was scary knowing that I had changed in front of people I grew up with, but I learned to stop caring.

The phrase "Free your mind" is often a cliché. We hear this term all the time but never apply it to our everyday life or look deeper into the actual meaning. The actual meaning is freeing your mind from the bondage imposed by outside forces and breaking out of the teachings that make us feel weak and unhealthy. Our freedom should never be sold in exchange for outside forces such as society, media, etc. Freedom, love, growth, and healing are all one, making it crucial to life's lessons; selling your freedom in order to return to the safety of bondage is also selling your love, growth, and recovery. With a clear sense of freedom, you'll be able to create and embrace healthy relationships. For example,—my passion is balancing my artistic, educational, and humanitarian vision because those things not only make me happy, they also make me free.

Life is not the problem; life without freedom is. Remain observant and uncertain of the direction that life takes you. Freedom will have no answer key, no map, and no direction. Every moment is now, and everything is new. When you seek the answer, the answer is now updated. When you look for the direction, the map has completely changed its course. The best way to officially be free is to be completely comfortable. You have lived your life constantly trying to fit in a realm of false ideologies, and not even knowing or accessing the full potential of your worth. It is time to let the chain slowly unwind. When the chain unwinds, you will know, and when the freedom takes over your mind, you have mastered the second step toward healing.

Acceptance

The acceptance of self can be quite problematic. We seek things we do not have simply because we are bored or crave something new. However, boredom of self is an excuse for uncertainty. When you want to be different because you are bored, you are uncertain of your true capability. When you want other people to be different ---- specifically, your partners, your friends, or your family members --- you are uncertain of your self-entitlement. We cannot be different, nor can the people around us be anything but themselves. Yes, we are constantly growing and evolving, but progressing and trying to be different are two separate things. Progression is the improvement of self, and the realization of the attributes that either hold us back or keep us moving forward. Progression is also about developing morality in order to be the best you. Being different is not progression. Our minds tend to believe we are trying to be different, but we are just purifying ourselves. When you grew up constantly eating sweets, then learned that eating sweets is not healthy for you, you learned right from wrong and progressed from that. When you told your first lie, you learned that the best thing to do is to be honest and you made progress when you realized that. We are the embodiment of our progression.

You will never be able to change yourself, but you can grow in ways that will positively affect your mind-set and outlook. You also will never be able to change others, although you can have an effect on them.

Change is nonexistent. It is only an illusion, like the love/hate phenomenon.

Imagine hating someone. When you hate, what happens internally? What does your mind want to do to those people? You want them to be as far away as possible. You develop a destructive mind-set toward them. You would like them to disappear and to exist no more — you think negatively.

Imagine loving someone. When you love others, what happens internally? You care about them and want to protect them. You will not allow anything bad to happen to them. You want the love to be immortal--- you think positively.

Look at both situations. Even though they are opposites, they both are two opposing elements of the same flower. Love is creative. Hate is destructive. No creation is possible without destruction; no destruction is worth something unless it is for creation.

Accepting yourself is like love and hate. Your past and your present practically embody polar opposites. You assume the present has nothing to do with the past. You love your current position but hate who you used to be. You want to destroy the past and create your future. Everything is connected and one cannot exist without the other. Changing self will not cure you of all of your forms of the past, present, and future. Past, present, and future are one. Accepting self as a whole will make you heal because you can only be one with yourself and one is to all, as all is to one.

Acceptance is not resignation, change is. Change is the desire to be perfect. Acceptance is embracing all of your imperfections. Never forget what made you the person you are today, and be willing to fully forgive your past. Forgiveness is not a sign of weakness: it is for you. When you do not forgive yourself, your past is holding the power over you and you are not accepting it in its entirety. When you do not forgive the people who have harmed you, they hold their power over you and you have not accepted the past in its entirety.

Believe in the law of connection. Everything connects to something and every connection will benefit from something. Observe and document your progress. Understand that your pain is not weakness and that it comes with progress. Connect every situation you have experienced and accept that you cannot change what happened. You can only make something good out of it. Acceptance is the key to progression, for progression is the result of healing.

Your mind wants what it wants, but your soul needs what it needs. Change your mind-set to connect with your soul and move in a direction that will benefit you. Always realize that the biggest downfall is ignoring our soul's needs. Our purpose will find its way when we let go of guilt from the past and find freedom in the present.

Mind, body, and soul are all connected. Past, present, and future are all connected. Healing connects to all.

Love: *Dear Self, Dear Partner, Dear Passion. Can I call each*

Home?

"The confusion between the idea of love and the reality of love creates misguided youth. The meaning of love is so powerful, yet it is misinterpreted to the point where we believe love has only one purpose."

—

April Okorie

Society has taught us how we are supposed to "love". It tells us that one day we will grow up to meet the person who completes us, the person who is our counterpart, our other half. Although we live by this mantra in hopes of finding our "true love," this concept is very disturbing and impairs the minds of humans as early as their childhood. We do not know how to love because we are raised to put a title on something so intricate and much more profound than a simple-minded view. For years we absorb everything we are taught. We live by the directions and teachings of others and forget the foundation of our own beliefs. We repeat the same cycle and teach our children unspoken instructions given by society. They, in turn, teach their children how to live and love. Everything becomes so forced that self-love becomes anomaly. Some people are never taught to express themselves, express their love, or how to control their own love.

Love of Self

We hear the expression "We must love ourselves before we allow another person to love us," but we never actually apply it to our everyday lives. Attraction equates to self-reflection. We unconsciously attract people who are a reflection of us, not just through sensual affection, but metaphysical bonding. If we do not know ourselves enough to love each aspect of ourselves as a whole, how can we love another person?

Every individual has their own personal laws, a set of laws and morals. Take siblings, for instance. Both have the same upbringing, both share the same belief systems due to the teachings of their parents, but one sibling is very different from another because of their different personalities and perspectives. It is not just the palm of our hands and the tips of our fingers that have fingerprints; our psychic apparatus has a mental fingerprint separating our selfhood from everyone else in the world. No two people on this earth are exactly the same. This is why there are people in the world that reflect our personality, but not our identification. There are also people in our lives that share our same beliefs, but do not replicate our selfhood.

Companionship and romantic compatibility has a lot to do with this ideal. Why do we ask our love interests what music they like or what their goals are? We want to know that they are on our wavelength. We want to know that they are driven and intrigued by the same emotional experiences so we can trust that they will understand our pain, our happiness, our interests, and our dislikes. But this can be easily fabricated. All one has to do is listen to someone discuss their inner thoughts with passion and then find something from their own experience that is similar emotionally and share it. The heart we allowed to open freely, fell for the trap of allowing someone unfaithful into our lives. We sometimes fall for traps and become attracted to a counterfeit love.

The problem begins with the story and the problem escalates when we become romantically attracted to people who were not on our wavelength. This means people who were never right for you but had something you respected, or admired and desired. You wanted to be with the other person in order to fill a void inside of yourself, to feel good about your character, or to change a situation in your life. You believed forcing love was the answer to all of your problems, but never realized the amount of energy it took to maintain a relationship that's not good for you.

Do you like yourself? Do the people in your life mirror you in terms of philosophical views, work ethic, etc.? If they mirror your persona, you know that the relationship is not perfect. To a certain extent, stress and disagreements are healthy, but overall the bond is unbreakable. When you think of the people who naturally come into your life, the ones with the same interests and perspective as you, are you attracted to them? When you find honesty within yourself, you will realize that the things you do not like about the people you surround yourself with, are the things you do not like about yourself. You constantly reject natural attraction and look for the qualities you want to see in yourself in somebody else.

There is only one solution that will set you free. You must be willing to learn how to love yourself, and you must appreciate your growth and gradually evolve into the person you want to become. One way to think well of yourself is to realize that perfection can never be obtained. No one on earth does things quite like you, no one sees the world the same way, and no one has your talents, ambitions, or skills. No one makes the same mistakes or the same comments. Once you adopt this ideology, you will see love through freedom. You will diminish the idea of toxic love and create a love that works immensely for you.

Before we go more in depth about loving another person, we must find the root of our spirituality; we must start by asking, "What is self-love?" There are two main kinds of self-love: egocentric and spiritual. Both feed off each other, but only one of them is beneficial. Although, self-love merely means "love of self," it is more complex and multilayered. Egocentric self-love is from the ego and is about self-protection and survival. Ego is the physical aspect of our love for self ---- how others view our life, and what we see about our life. Ego self-love seeks approval and respect, and fears rejection. When life is not what we wish it to be, egocentric self-love weakens, and the more out of place we feel with our life, the more the self-love diminishes. As it weakens, self-hate begins, and we do not love ourselves until we secure what we believe is perfect.

On the other hand, spiritual self-love is never-ending. It connects the spirit, mind, body, and soul instead of neglecting the dire needs of each. It loves regardless of your health or appearance, or whatever adversity you face. It cares about the well-being of your whole self; it allows you to heal all wounds and complete love. Spiritual self-love is the forbidden fruit of life. Society does not teach us this kind of love because it defies all social norms, like when society turns left and you turn right. Learn and understand that spiritual self-love is raw, explicit, and a fresh awakening of being your true self. The root of love is spiritual love because it is the deepest, purest source available. This love that is beyond the human love is more fulfilling, and once the root of our love is conquered, we can love another wholeheartedly.

Love of Partner

What makes someone love me? If someone does this or is this way, it means they love me. What must someone do to show that they love you? Answer these questions as honestly as possible. (Space provided below)

These are our inner rules; the art of limiting our time, capacity, and energy in order to either give or receive love. With the rules you just made, you simplified human love to a guideline. The rules we have about love are well-intentioned, but they stifle our spiritual boundaries. It is natural to have a preference, but completely disregarding someone because they do not fit your dictates of conscience is the problem. We want other people to love us as we are and we never settle for anyone who won't accept us, but we put multiple conditions on what love is or how our love was meant to be.

Spiritual love has no boundaries. Human love is a construct. Human love sees with the eyes. Spiritual love sees beyond. This deep, unlimited connection is often called a "soul mate" in our culture. Nothing is wrong with romantic movies ---- they are actually quite appealing----but the true meaning of a "soul mate" is deeper. When we base it on perceptions from movies, then we do not see that there are requirements to keep the relationship balanced.

Explore the nature of relationships. Understand that the chemistry and variations of a relationship help us to better balance all of our commitments. Correlating a person to being a soul mate when everything in the relationship goes smoothly is false. Even soul-mate relationships have hardships to overcome. Once you understand the types of relationships that exist, you will be able to move ahead and find the person who matches you down to the toes of your soul.

"Buddhists say that if you meet somebody and your heart pounds and your knees go weak, they are not the one. When you do meet your soulmate, you'll feel calm."

The power of finding our spiritual mate is natural and magnetic. When you put two magnets together, they repel each other. They are two complete things that share a common power in the center. The magnetic friction represents the two complete and strong forces that are independent on their own. The force and power between them symbolizes the connection of the souls intertwining.

After you find "the one," the demand for security increases. You do not want to be hurt or to lose the powerful connection. This is an important stepping stone and a new level in the relationship. One thing I have noticed in bonding of any kind is the need to feel safe. When you do not know what the other person thinks about you, it creates sorrow and fear; this is due to a lack of security. The involuntary need for security invites insecurity. Being with an individual, helping each other, and being psychologically nourished by another creates anxiety and fear because you do not want to lose that dependence. But do you demand to be safe simply because you cannot be safe alone?

Love needs individual solitude. Everyone needs time to themselves moments before they lose themselves in a relationship. We only develop fear when we are afraid to be alone; we fear that we won't be fine if we lose our partner. Love is not a product of pleasure and everything a relationship offers. You can give love to yourself. You can give yourself security and emotional assurance. If you have solitude in a relationship, you will have the reassurance of the power you possess with your sole identity.

Another reason we cling to safety in a relationship is a lack of openness. Secrecy and love are polar opposites, but we will never be able to know what someone is thinking. We can only trust them to be open and vice versa. As individuals, we tend to cherish our inner thoughts because they mean the universe to us and they are our personal memoir. Secrecy is important for outside forces simply because everyone does not need to know our next move; privacy allows us to be one in our growth. Secrecy within a relationship destroys it because you are connected to your partner. You are one, and the love you share is one in spirit. It is hard to be open, but love knows when you have met your soul mate. We always want to be in power and control of our own identity.

Imagine giving someone the key to unlock the vaults of your mind, and they know your guilty pleasures and your darkest thoughts. You would probably be devastated. Switch the scenario to your partner.

Imagine not knowing your partner's deepest thoughts: what makes them inconsolable, what makes them happy, what gives them strength. This would make you feel helpless and vulnerable.

Secrecy leads to confusion and lack of communication between each other. Without knowing it, our ego takes over. We try to overpower our partner by preserving our own secrets and then it becomes a competitive disaster. Secrets in general mean something you want to hide, something that you are not ready to share or never will share. A relationship is a combination of mutual trust and understanding, so keeping a secret equates to a lack of trust. You will know when the person is right for you, and that you have a soul connection because it will lead to openness and fearlessness. This will also lead to knowing that you will never need to lose yourself in someone else.

We are aware that relationships take effort, but we actually never prepare ourselves for when it gets hard. When the relationship becomes difficult, we usually point the finger at our partner and miss the opportunity to face the fear that exists within us. Love and fear cannot coexist. With mutual openness and individual security, there is love; with the demand to be safe with secrecy, there is fear. Do you love? Or do you fear?

Love of Passion

Passion is a state of being. It is also a temporary euphoria. Of course, we all wish it would last forever, but the fact is that it doesn't. If passion lasted forever, we would not be able to accomplish anything. We do not even realize that we love the rush.

Back in the beginning of high school, after months of being tormented by others, I wanted to help victims of bullying. I wanted to help people who felt suicidal, as if their world could not be repaired, because I was able to help myself. This was at the age of fifteen and I was debating whether I was too young. The idea that "age does not define maturity" ran through my head, which is true in most cases, so I marched in anti-bullying parades, I joined the anti-bullying club at my school, and I donated money to humanitarian causes thinking that I would change the world through protests and activism. Even though these things raise awareness, I felt as though I was not doing enough. I wanted to truly impact the lives of others and, let them know that it will get better, but what I was doing was not leading in that direction.

After a while, I stopped. The bullying resumed, but not as badly as during my ninth-grade year of high school. I started to become depressed again. I was constantly in pain. This situation happened on and off until I sought out self-love. This time around, I knew for sure that my depression was over and that I wanted to resume helping people, but I did not want to keep protesting. I decided to seek solitude and read more books to educate myself on self-improvement in order to make sure I did not go through this again. I had to help myself before I could help others.

One day I attended a seminar about radical transformation. The teacher would travel around the world helping others and spreading his teachings in Igbo and English. I attended the seminar because I had one mission: waking up to full consciousness through a fundamental inner revolution. I learned to meditate, to become still, to love silence, and to calm my mind. But I also learned to open up my passion for love and for life; I learned to open up my heart. I renewed and learned to sacrifice in order to become my true self. This is why I emphasize that age has nothing to do with maturity---your heart will know when you are ready to mature.

The main point of the seminar was that you have to first clean up your personal house before you clean anyone else's. The transformation I was looking for had to happen inside of me, and I was the only one who could make it happen.

Having a heart is scary. It needs to be managed well. The heart is the source of great joy and happiness, yet at the same time, it can be the source of sorrow. We can do much good when our hearts are open and filled with positivity but we can do so much damage when they are closed and filled with negativity. The heart lets us be more authentic and less reactive, and thus be more efficient agents for spiritual activism. Once we can accomplish spiritual activism for ourselves, it can be done for others.

The seminar emphasized renewal and cleansing. How do you expect to spread love and embrace your passion when your love for yourself is not even sufficient? The power is within you to channel your heart's direction. With life's challenges, it can be hard to stay open. Our tendency is to put a shield of protection and defensiveness around our heart. This stops us from experiencing and spreading love.

We attach to things that have no relevance to our being. There are so many opportunities of oneness and connection, but we choose to love the things that end up draining our energy. There are so many things that can change the world, things that are right in front of us.

What actually disconnects us from our passions?

Disconnection stems from separation of love of self from love of others. We also disconnect ourselves because we believe we have to do everything on our own. We are under the cultural idealization that we are heroes if we are strong and hardcore individualists. Self-reliance is an overvalued concept, but it has been deemed as highly respectable. To do something for others or to need something from others is seen as needy and weak. We resist from helping other people because it is a sign of weakness.

When I was being bullied, a lot of people would tell me behind closed doors that they felt badly for me, but out in the open they would not do anything when they saw my pain. They did not want to be seen as weak or have their respectability affected. We should always go with our instincts. If we feel that the right thing to do is to help someone, help them. The desire to help them is the love that's in your heart. It does not want to be shielded, but to be expressed.

We avoid needing anybody. When we feel that need, we immediately feel ashamed and we deny it, for it brings up past wounds. Love of self and solitude is very important, but you cannot separate yourself from the rest of the world due to pain. So how do we open our hearts to others after years of masking them takes practice and it needs a bit of courage. Just as we develop awareness and mindfulness through meditation, we can develop wholeness by paying attention to our hearts and listening within. Allowing ourselves to feel all that is there slowly gives us room to open up. Acceptance of what is there creates a true ground for experiencing our feelings. To allow our fears and hurts to speak to us enables us to experience a much deeper sense of compassion and empathy.

Being passionate about something is when that something causes you to have an extreme emotional response. It can be either negative or positive. Love is passion and it connects to how we react in life. Love connects us to all; love makes us feel peaceful, clear, and balanced. Acting on love allows us to be calm and help others, help our partners and help ourselves. Love always creates win-win solutions no matter what type of love it is. When difficulties arise, patience and love resolve them. You become flexible with everyone you know, and you open yourself up to many opportunities that help you help yourself. Love allows us to step out of our comfort zone and makes it easier for us to take risks regarding our love. Love is oxygen for your mind and soul. The more connected you are with love, the healthier you will be mentally and physically. Love is all things possible.

Prosper: *Spiritual Advancing and Self-Liberation*

"To say the words 'I am free' is meaningless without action. Being free should be felt"

- April Okorie

In order to be successful in anything you do, you need to establish your own definition of achievement. After you define what success means for you, your achievements will follow. Many people focus on success in a broader sense rather than on what success means for themselves. People also believe success is only available in one aspect of their lives, such as their career choice or goals; that is why they struggle in other areas. Success and progression are not trade-offs. We consciously neglect one or more aspects of our life in order to succeed in another; for example, neglecting your family to have a successful job. Everyone in your field sees you as extremely successful, but your family feels abandoned.

All areas of your life should be successful. Profession leads to success, and it is your own interpretation. Progression is a state of mind because we all interpret success differently. Regardless of our own personal interpretation of growth, we all advance spiritually. To advance spiritually is to get to know your true self, the one you see in the mirror that is more than your physical appearance.

Spiritual advancement is a way to learn what it is you came to accomplish on this earth. Before we were able to heal, we suffered, and before we were able to free our minds, we were caged. Each phenomenon correlates to our philosophical mantra. The opportunities are limitless when we give up all ego, desires, and temptations.

Spiritual advancement begins when there is a revolutionary change in ego and self-reflection. One must live from the soul, and even if specific pursuits are not directly connected to the soul, the ultimate motive would be to do things right by your soul. When maintenance of the body and soul becomes a top priority you will be able to realize your higher purpose. In order to advance, one must be willing to break down their purpose in an unconscious love-and-hate world.

We share the universe with lower and higher universal energy. The lower wavelengths are associated with darkness----negative souls who refuse to see the light. These lower wavelengths move away from the light that shines in their direction, and they create negative energy everywhere they go. The higher wavelengths seek the light. They are drawn to it like the air they breathe.

You create your journey with what you think, how you feel, and how you act. The more negative you are, the more connected you will be to the low wavelength. You will attract people of the same vibrational pathway, and your spiritual advancement will diminish. The more positive you are, the more connected you will be with the higher wavelengths, which will attract people who are more positive.

Each individual is on a different level of spiritual advancement because we all have different experiences and individualistic pathways. The purpose of life is to move toward the level of positive vibrations. If a person does not do this, they will experience a series of purifying events until they see the light. Everyone is striving to move forward for their own benefit. Achieving spiritual advancement provides physical benefits. As you advance, your body will advance at the same pace. You will notice that the signs of aging are slowed, your health improves, you feel calm, and you handle situations in a different way because you are at peace with yourself. Your body psychologically knows that it is calm and nothing can affect its positive state.

It is hard to achieve calmness because people on the other end of the spectrum (on the negative wavelength) always try to influence those who think differently from them, and make those people believe in their way of life. Once someone adopts this negative behavior, it is hard for them to return to behave as their true, loving selves. The goal should be protection. Do not be naive, do not follow anything against your intuition, and do not lose yourself. Spirituality involves the purification of oneself to allow for the liberation of the soul so it can become full of positivity.

A life of prosperity is a goal that many people want to reach. Most people want to be prosperous without healing any prolonged damage they have sustained. That is the problem.

The Five Cardinal Rules of Spiritual Advancement

1. Never lie to yourself.

When you lie to yourself, you are bound to lie to others. Lying creates an unhealthy life and causes you to redirect your own destiny. Hear your truth, be your truth, and speak your truth.

2. Never wish harm to anyone, even if a person has harmed you. They have to achieve spiritual advancement on their own and purify themselves. Focus on your own journey.

One denounces others in order to hide their own insecurities. Wishing people harm or putting others down automatically makes you feel better because lowering the value of others makes you feel better about yourself. If you wish harm upon others, you are not in total control of your own life. People who are satisfied with their lives do not wish to harm other people because it makes no sense-----destruction has no relation to positivity.

3. Be patient. The best things come when we allow ourselves to embrace the journey.

We feel the need to rush things and to rush our destiny. As you move through life, patience is the factor that helps you maintain authenticity.

4. Do not seek approval or expect anything from people.

The ego is very insecure and requires validation of its doubts. We seek approval because we have not let go of our ego. I suspect that part of the reason is for our own protection.

Approval-seeking behaviors come from fear of disapproval. Get rid of the thought of not being good enough. Disapproval and negativity are part of life. It is all about how you deal with each situation.

5. Humility and hospitality will take you far.

Sharing your spiritual home with others shows inner generosity and demonstrates your character. This will help you advance because you are proving to yourself that you do not need to receive something in order to be kind.

Humans tend to go against these rules. They wind up never content with their life or depressed because they make prosperity about greed. Greed is usually driven by a sense of deprivation; it is a survival instinct and a need to compete. Although we do not know what our circumstances will be in the future, we must never lose ourselves in greed.

We create a mentality that we will not be successful or content unless we have more, and that we will never get what we want or we will lose all we have worked for if we do not fight for what we have. But being greedy violates the cardinal rules. The mentality of greed is based on fear and perpetuates our problems. We never believe that we have advanced and that we still need to fight, which creates a vicious cycle that cannot be broken without changing our perspective.

How can we get in touch with our spiritual soul, our intuition?

Meditate on a situation that happened in the past. Once you determine the root of the problem, take these steps:

1. Reflect

Give yourself the credit you deserve just for living, for being. Reflect on all of the time and energy you have spent creating a life that's perfect for you. Remember all the struggling, healing, suffering, discovering, working, succeeding, and failing---feeling frustration, joy, disappointment, love, and hurt in order to be right where you are in the present moment. Reflect on the past and the present in order to, build the best future.

2. Recognize

Recognize all of the effort you have put into living your life and what you have learned along the way—the good and the bad. Nobody knows your experience in depth but you. Notice that there is no mention of learning from just the "good" parts of your life—all of your life has value.

3. Reconcile

Look at your life in the present moment and give yourself credit for your efforts, without reservation. We need to be honest about who we are and accept ourselves as completely as possible, including the things we think are wrong or bad. Self-acceptance is not a judgment that everything is the way you want it to be; it is a decision to accept and honor yourself as you are, so that you can move forward in a positive manner.

4. Reserve Spirit.

When we make peace with self, we naturally, become aware of our spirit. Our spirit is our core, the thriving part of us. We don't have to go looking for it, because it is always with us. Each period of our lives has a meaning, a meaning that shapes our identity. The advancement of spirit allows us to choose the direction we want our life to follow and how we choose to view the world.

Cleanse your soul. Do not let the world make your heart turn cold. Love yourself and those around you. Free your mind from ideas that do not conform with your true self. Be yourself. Treat your body, mind, and soul correctly and prosperity will come.

"I had the goal to design the life I felt I needed in order to survive in my own cocoon, once finding its true meaning and my true purpose, I never looked back. I choose me today, I choose me every day. I choose to heal. I choose to love. I choose to prosper."

-April Okorie

Words for All

This section is solely displaying some of my personal poetry, spoken words, self-documents that I want to share with the world.

Allow me to touch you and leave you with a deep part of my mind

Coping through the psycho analysis of my mind, you travel through its vaults

You gain insight, and impact a lost soul

Deep in my body lies the blood that flows and circulates elation

Hoping that a simple touch from skin to skin can spark a brain that will shine a light in the world

I will pass on my warmth, as you pass on the knowledge of solidarity

It all starts with a simple touch from the gentle skin

When innocence dies, the world turns cold. As babies we were born off of innocence, often curious to know how the river flows, or why it rains. As we grow, we build immunity to this world, often seeing differences as detrimental instead of beautiful. I often reminisce with my thoughts and develop a deplorable sensation of sadness. Knowing that love decreases while hate expands. One thing we share is this ravishing universe, why not create peace?

Be curious, stay curious

When it rains

I like to believe that earth is cleansing itself from the waste

The bare earth cries a song of relaxation

And when you listen closely to the rain it is like a rhythm

I call this rhythm Earth's music

Sometimes our soul needs healing to repair itself; like earth with rain

Be your own remedy

They say good and evil are in the power of the tongue

It was some words that turned us cold

Some words that made our spirit warm.

Each word has a different meaning that can be interpreted by the

listener.

Choose each word wisely

You have examined all portions of self

You have examined yourself over and over

Nothing can turn you away from the love you have detected

The inner choices can free us from despair

The courage to move on can heal our being

The desire to live in love instead of fear can silence the doubt

Diminish the fear; become fearless

Free yourself from the need for approval every step of the journey

The origin of your contentment should be from the truthfulness you are to yourself when in solitude

Allow people to depart physically if they do not support your journey

Even if done alone, allow your inner self to be loved, supported, and seen

Show and tell the truth about yourself through expressions, actions, and what you create

The quiet moments are where we can observe the full range of our emotions

The good and bad, the beautiful flaws that define us and the past that improve us

We fall in love with the wholeness

Often we ask for growth, but we do not want to go through the lessons necessary to achieve it. "The easy way out" or "the quickest way possible" is our ultimate initiative, but we realized it does not work. The necessary part of growth is discomfort.

My Philosophy #1: I will always move forward. I will know myself as well as the people around me. Although it is good to receive recognition, I will never allow that to change my outlook on life. I will always do my best to give, share my warmth with others, pass on the positive spirituality, and touch a lost soul. I will do my best to honor whatever my soul presents to me.

Perfection was your reason and it pursued you

Acceptance was your reasoning and it disappointed you

Security was your reason and it bored you

We often chase after our ideal perfection only to realize that perfection is nonexistent

It scares us from continuing to try

As soon as you remove the idea of perfection, you will realize that it was the acceptance and security that made you who you are today

That is the deepest and purest truth and it is also the darkest truth that makes us a real genuine person

You will start to see yourself as an individual instead of a product

You started out with the perfection ideal, realized that is not reality, and then become real

This is one of many passages I wrote during a period of depression and self-hate. I wrote this during my ninth-grade year of high school. I was bullied throughout my school years, but ninth grade was when it reached another level that shook me to a point of no return.

May 13, 2013

I don't know what I hate more: the people who openly hate me and continue to harass me, or the people who secretly hate me but act like they don't. I want to write out my feelings because they always say it helps. I guess the theme of my writing today is pain because that is all I have been feeling lately. I barely have clear eyes anymore, and I never smile. My heart, my life, is just pain.

I keep feeling like I'm falling down for some reason. My pain just keeps getting worse. It's no longer only at school; the pain I feel follows me and haunts me even outside of school now. I wake up screaming and crying in the middle of the night, but I guess my family is immune to it since they sleep through it nowadays, except for my mother. "It's just that their words keep haunting me, Mommy," I keep telling her every night. These people claim they don't care about me and I am irrelevant but keep making my life miserable. Are they happy now?

It's really funny—today at school, I lost another friend! And her words were, "I can't be friends with you anymore. You get into too much drama." I basically get this every day or have people avoid me because they're scared it will mess up their reputation. But with her, I poured my heart to her, told her what they did to me. I really thought she cared for me the most, and now I lost her because it's getting worse? I wish she knew that if she was also being bullied, I wouldn't have stopped being friends with her. But who needs friends…ha.

No one truly even knows me, and they keep treating me this way. I hate myself for not allowing my mom to report my harassers to the school board. Was I scared? No, but I believed that it will never get better for me.

Every single day of my life that I decide to wake up and go to school is and will be the worst day of my life.

Adore the expedition, not so much the outcome

Enrapture and appreciate every breath of air, every yes, every no

Every moment that allows you to live

I am April Nneka Okorie

 And

I am starving

Starving for growth

Starving for possibilities

Starving to conquer the aim for peace

Starving for a moment in my life where I can finally say I have reached

Home

Long before the birth of humans

Alluring was the beauty of Mother Earth.

Her diverse environments, her people

Hatred, Corruption, Poverty, and many more pivotal things changed and impaired her beauty

All, an exotic reflection of her biodiversity

Unlock the beauty

The closer we are to accepting differences and opening our hearts to love

The closer we are to Mother Earth's love

And she will come back greater and stronger

In the midst of letting go of things that hindered me most, I find myself latching back on to them.

It becomes a fight to find yourself in the midst of everything that life throws at you.

But it is a fight I am willing to endure.

Forever

The strange battle between the old and the new "me" always seemed to be a catastrophic one

I learned to release my old and stubborn ability to pity myself

It started to feel strange to let that part of me go

But it was even stranger watching myself struggle with that pain

It had to be gone

I am digging very deep to find my next level of life

Feeling very bashful about it

Hungry for it

And giving all my energy to it because I was telling myself that this is only the beginning

And it is

"A friend is a reflection of who you are" they always say

When you notice that your friends do not embody who you are as a person; if they do not motivate you, if they do not provide you with constructive criticism, then reevaluate who you are sharing your life and time with

Bring on the beginning of your new journey with people that truly define your character

People who bring out the happiness and spiritual euphoria; your growth does not feel stumped by these people

Though it hurts at times

It is better to show your authentic self and be ignored

Than to be praised for being what others want you to be

Let Go

Move forward

Love today, love every day, Love always

My Philosophy #2: You may search your whole life looking for answers, believing that they will heal you, and you may also search your whole life trying to prove yourself to people who hurt you in the past. Know that not everything in life needs proper closure. Life was not meant to be very easy. It was meant to be a series of journeys in order to reach the full potential of self—a self that is phenomenal and untouchable. Every end simply means a new beginning.

32084138R00046

Made in the USA
Middletown, DE
22 May 2016